I can see a pink tongue!
I wonder who that belongs to?

إِنّي أَرى لِساناً زَهْرِيَّ ٱللون!

لِمَنْ ياتُرى ذلك ٱللسان ؟

'It's mine!' says the tiger.
'I lap water from
the river with it.'

« إِنَّهُ لي ! » قَال ٱلنَّمِر.
« فَأَنا أَلْعَقُ
ٱلماءَ بِه . »

I can see a long nose!
I wonder who that belongs to?
إنّي أَرى أَنْفاً طَويلاً !
لِمَن ياتُرى ذلك ٱلأَنف ؟

'It's mine!' says the elephant.
'I hold things with it.'

« إِنَّهُ لي ! » قالَ ٱلفيل .
« أَنا أَرفَعُ ٱلأَشْياءَ بِهِ . »

I can see a long neck!
I wonder who that belongs to?

إنّي أَرى عُنُقاً طَويلاً !
لِمَنْ ياتُرى ذلك ٱلعُنُق ؟

‘It’s mine!’ says the giraffe.
‘I reach high leaves with it.’

« إِنَّهُ لي ! » قَالَت ٱلزَّرافَة .
« إِنّي أَصِلُ أَوْراقَ ٱلشّجَرِ ٱلعالِيَةِ به . »

I can see a green tail!
I wonder who that belongs to?

إِنِّي أَرى ذَيْلاً أَخْضَر !

لِمَنْ ياتُرى ذَلكَ ٱلذّيل ؟

'It's mine!' says the crocodile.
'I swim in the river with it.'

« إِنَّهُ لي ! » قال ٱلتِّمْساح .
« إِنّي أَسْبَحُ بِهِ في ٱلنَّهر . »

I can see a furry paw!
I wonder who that belongs to?

إنّي أرى كَفَّ حَيوانٍ مَكْسُواً بٱلفِراء !

لِمَنْ ياتُرى ذَلك ٱلكَفّ ؟

‘It’s mine!’ says the bear.
‘I scoop out honey with it.’

« إِنَّهُ لي ! » قال ٱلدُبّ .
« أَنا أَغرِفُ ٱلعَسَلَ بِهِ . »

I can see a wriggly body!
I wonder who that belongs to?

إنّي أرى جِسْماً يَتَلَوّى !

جِسْمُ مَنْ ذلك ياتُرى ؟

'It's mine!' says the snake.
'I slide through the grass with it.'

« إِنَّهُ لي ! » قال ٱلثُّعبان .
« إِنِّي أَزْحَفُ بَيْنَ ٱلحَشائِشِ بِهِ . »

I can see a curly tail!
I wonder who that belongs to?

إنّي أَرى ذَنَباً مَعْقُوصاً !

لِمَنْ ياتُرى ذلك ٱلذَّنَب ؟

'It's mine!' says the monkey.
'I hang from branches with it.'

« إِنَّهُ لي ! » قال ٱلقِرْد .
« أَنا أَتَعَلَّقُ على ٱلأَغْصانِ بِه . »

I can see a small round eye!
I wonder who that belongs to?

إنّي أَرى عَيْناً صَغيرَةً مُسْتَدِيرَة !

لِمَنْ تِلْكَ ٱلعَيْنُ ياتُرى ؟

‘It’s mine!’ says the parrot.
‘I watch out for
hungry lions with it.’

« إِنَّها لي ! » قالَت ٱلبَبَّغاء .
« إِنّي أُراقِبُ بِها
ٱلأُسُودَ ٱلجائِعَة . »

And just around the corner,
I can see a big red mouth with sharp teeth!
I wonder who that belongs to?

وَقُرْبَ ٱلمُنْعَطَفِ
إنّي أرى فَماً كَبيراً أَحْمَرَ ذا أَسْنانٍ حَادَّة !
لِمَنْ ياتُرى ذَلِكَ ٱلفَم ؟

'It's mine!'
says the lion,
'and I'll eat
you up with it!'

« إِنَّهُ لي ! »
قَالَ ٱلأَسَد
« وَبِه
سَأَبْتَلِعُكَ ! »

Help! We'd better run as fast as we can!

يَامَنْ يُساعِدُنا ! عَلَيْنا أَنْ نَجْرِيَ بِأَقْصى سُرْعَة !

Can you see all
the animals we met?

How many are there?